A Mitt

by Helena Hill
illustrated by Rémy Simard

Practice Decodable 12

McGraw Hill Education

Bothell, WA • Chicago, IL • Columbus, OH • New York, NY

MHEonline.com

Send all inquiries to:
McGraw-Hill Education
8787 Orion Place
Columbus, OH 43240

ISBN: 978-0-02-146272-8
MHID: 0-02-146272-0

Printed in China.

8 9 10 11 12 DSS 27 26 25 24 23

Tim had a tan mitt.

Had Sis hid it?

Did Dad have it?

Tim had a hint.

"It is on a hat stand," said Tim.

Dad can hand him a mitt.